john tottenham
the inertia variations

2010 EDITION

KEROSENE BOMB PUBLISHING

2010
kerosenebomb.com

The Inertia Variations

John Tottenham

SECOND EDITION MARCH 2010

Copyright © 2010

All rights reserved under International and Pan-American Copyright Conventions.
This publication is deemed inadmissable as evidence.

Library Of Congress Cataloging-in-Publication Data

Tottenham, John
Inertia Variations / John Tottenham

ISBN 0-9719977-9-9

1. Inertia, ennui, vacuity — Variations on. I. Title

Photograph Huxley Terrace , 2004
Art direction, Design, Andy Takakjian

KeroseneBomb Publishing
Los Angeles, CA 90041

kerosenebomb.com

Manufactured in the United States of America

it's a struggle to get one's ideas across

I

I lie on the sofa, stretched out like a corpse,
With eyes closed against the dying light,
Lulled by the silence beyond the waves
Of traffic. Until, eventually, the good- humor man,
On his last go-round, penetrates the fog,
And I resign myself to another final squandered
Afternoon: to not being able to function at this
Or any other time of day.

II

I cannot account for the hours
That have been smothered into
Submission. Not only this afternoon
But day after day, year after year.
Over the wasted course of which time
I have been repeating this futile lament:
That I can't go on like this. And this too:
That it makes no difference.

THE CHALLENGE

If I am not doing the work
That for some obscurely grasped reason
I believe it is my duty to perform,
Then I cannot, in its place,
Allow myself to do anything else
That is pleasurable or productive.
The main challenge, ultimately,
Is not to fall asleep during the afternoon.

IV

All the sanitary, gastronomical, social and compulsive
Matters have been attended to. There is nothing left now
But to do the work. Yet it is still early, only two-thirty:
There is still time to lie down for a short while.
At three-thirty I awake. At four-thirty I bestir myself,
Slide off the sofa and stagger into the bathroom,
Berating myself for the waste while accepting
That it is too late now, to do anything about it.

THE RITES OF INDOLENCE

Breathing in the stale draughts
That sift through the cracks in the sofa,
Slowly dreaming myself into a demoralized fog
That loosely resembles the conscious state.
Groggy with unneeded sleep, I approach the table
Wondering if there is any use, at this point,
In attempting to do anything .
Probably not. But the gesture, at least, must be made.

THE LEGACY

The leaden prostrations, the unkempt wanings, the piercing
Vagueness. The day is over. It has not yet begun.
Another one of those days: they can be instructive.
But at this late stage of my lack of development, they have served
Their purpose; I have received a full enough education
In that area. Just let it go, the way of all the others,
Adding to an already rich legacy
Of lost afternoons.

FEELINGS

I may as well face the fact
That I am no longer capable
Of doing what I once believed
I was capable of doing.
Not that I had any reason to assume
That I was capable of it.
It was just a feeling that I had.
And now I have a different feeling.

RUSH HOUR

I thought I was dead, but, after a few seconds, I realized
That I was lying on the floor. It wasn't dark yet
But the sound of the traffic indicated that it was around
The time of day when most people were driving
Home from work, too tired, following a day's honest
Employment, to do anything requiring much effort.
Picking myself up from the floor and stumbling
Into lukewarm confusion, I felt much the same way.

RIVETING TORPOR

It is remarkable how far I am prepared to go
In order to avoid doing the one thing that might
Provide satisfaction, and it is remarkable to consider
What I will do instead of it, purely for the pleasure
Of being dissatisfied. When it is merely a matter
Of sitting down for a few hours and dreaming
That something of value might eventually arise
From this routine of self-enforced boredom.

X

I haven't been anywhere
In the world. And out of all the things
I could have done on this day, among
Others, that might have been fun, edifying
Or charitable, I have chosen instead
To sink somewhere in flustered haze.
As if anything might be salvaged
From these uselessly plumbed depths.

DRONING

Through this hot haze of overflowing
Undertow. Unspun through layers
Of numbness, I open my eyes to a quivering
Of specks and scintillas that fills the room.
In a state of dazed wonderment I dimly recognize
The fact that I have spent the entire afternoon asleep.
An achievement of sorts, made all the more impressive
By the full nine hours I received last night and this morning.

ART AND EROS

Often, around the middle of a week day afternoon,
I find myself considering the connection
Between sexual and creative energy.
Torn by futile lusts, I seek refuge
From the vagueness of the day
And the promise of endeavor
In reliable memories and fantasies
That spill, reliably, into sleep.

ANOMIC OTIOSITY

Dulling my senses with baths, naps,
Assorted languishings. For many years
I have sat down to do the work
That the world will be no worse off
Without, and I have not done the work.
And the world is no worse off. Just because
I haven't done anything with my life,
Does that make me a lesser man?

FIGMENT TO FILAMENT

Embracing reality unprepared,
Unbenumbed and unknown to myself.
Thrust from gratuitous haze into piercing recognition
Of the sudden uncomfortable fact that this life is mine
Only. And this is what I have chosen to do with it.
A fleeting clarity, a sense of exposure, a liability.
It lasts only a few seconds, seems too much to bear,
And disappears.

THE DAILY GRIND

Every day some fresh hindrance I pursue.
Sometimes not so fresh.
Usually, in fact, the opposite.
That is to say, the same
Systematic dulling of the mind
That occupies most of my afternoons.
Thwarting satisfaction may be harder work,
For all I know, than the thwarted work itself.

A ROUGH DAY

I ate too much chocolate and fell asleep on the sofa.
And remained there.
After a while I rose. I sat down at the table for a few minutes.
Out of focus, unable to give of myself : I couldn't
Stay there. I retreated again to the sofa and
Lay there until darkness filled the room.
A rough day, I thought: as rough as a day can be
Without leaving chair or sofa.

THE ARRIVAL

For years on end I have been sitting here
Impatiently awaiting potency; some explosive revelatory surge
That will carry me away and permit no looking back.
But this moment of deliverance has not arrived,
And I have done nothing to hasten it.
Perhaps it doesn't matter.
Perhaps I wasn't meant to do anything:
In which case, I have succeeded admirably.

XVIII

In this reckless seasoned state,
I must hunt stealthily
For new sources of irritation,
Opportunities for evasion, and
Excuses for inanition. Yet wasted
Time somehow brings me around
To a keener understanding of a discipline
That will not be submitted to.

XIX

I do not know the meaning of hard work.
But I know what it means to adhere
To a schedule of diligent work-avoidance
As if it were a regular job: a strict routine
Of wandering around and lying down,
And brooding over wasted time.
I don't like to mix business
With anything, least of all pleasure.

SHIFT - WORK

It is six o'clock in the evening.
I have been awake for eight hours
But I cannot account for them.
Doing nothing: otherwise known
As preparing to work. It can go on
For a long time: years, even a lifetime.
There are not enough hours in the day
To accomodate my idleness.

NOTHING

When I ask someone what they are doing and they tell me
They are doing nothing, they are, in fact, usually doing
Something. Whereas if someone asks me what I am doing
And I tell them I am doing nothing, I am, in fact, actually doing
Nothing. Few people, outside jails or hospitals, have spent more
Time lying on a bed looking at a wall. Or on a sofa, or in a chair,
Or on a floor. Or looking at a floor, or a ceiling.
Or with eyes shut.

BEAUTY

The grace of an afternoon's promise
Has been denied.
The soft violet clouds drifting across the evening sky
Are lost on me.
I am too perturbed by the burden of wasted time,
And by the fact that my trousers are wrinkled
From lying upon the sofa for so long,
To appreciate such beauty.

RAGE TO LIVE

I lack the rage, or even the urge
To communicate. The reward of indolence
That indolently I strive towards
Holds me more than any furtive undertaking.
I can barely wait to be done
With this pretending to try
And move on
To not trying at all.

AT LEAST

I'm sitting here. At least I'm not
Supine. And if I succeed, no matter how
Fruitlessly and uneasily, in remaining
Here for another twenty minutes,
Then I will allow myself to return
To the sofa and close my eyes.
But it is highly unlikely
That I'll hold out for that long.

THE SHADOWS OF PURPOSE

Slowly, sleepily, shapelessly,
The afternoons have passed.
I have served my time
In the land of lost moments.
Much has been sacrificed
For this fit of abstraction
That has lasted a lifetime, so far.
Much that should be honored.

A MONDAY IN NOVEMBER

No,
I didn't do any work today.
But I thought about it for a moment,
Before lying down again
To bask in the wan light of decreation
And savor the fact
That I will not always be free
To ponder abstractions.

SUBMISSION

Finally, I summon the wherewithal
To stagger across the room. The moment
Has arrived for which the morning and most
Of the afternoon have been sacrificed
In a fitful blur. I drag myself to the table and slow down
Even further. Until the siren song of the sofa calls out.
And I am struck again by how much time I waste
Preparing to waste time.

THE PRIME OF LIFE

For a long time failure was something I strove for,
Shuffling timorously towards it, engaging in a form
Of shiftless brinksmanship, while imagining
That in the end I would avert it with an explosive charge.
But now, in the prime of my life, I have at last succeeded
In reaching the level where failure is no longer a matter of flirtation;
And the closer I gaze into the face of it, the more I consider
Not only death, but procreation.

RUINOUS TRANQUILITY

Shadows swathe and slash the ceiling.
Twisting ribbons of light suck dust through dirty rustling curtains.
In the lull of afterglow, with the residue of self-wrought congress
Caked upon my belly, I let fall the threadbare reins of conscience
And consciousness, and like a leaf surrendering to the wind,
Drift peacefully into the ether - to awake eventually and guiltily,
Knowing that it is too late to do anything,
That it is quite beyond me now.

XXX

Out of perversity, idleness, cowardice, fatalism and integrity,
I have chosen to shun my true path.
Despite it all, I have developed, in my time,
A certain unavoidable attachment to my life
And my ways: The chronic circlings between frustration
And inertia somehow comfort me, and, in the end,
I would rather be myself than anybody else.
Still, I suppose most people feel that way.

SOME SOFT SURFACE

This is no place for genteel shabbiness
Or dignified otiosity. The cushion is torn
And gray. One arm wreathes around it,
While the other hangs over the sofa's edge.
I awake again to a day that never started,
Embracing reality by sluggish degrees.
But perhaps reality is the wrong word,
And, in any event, it will not be embraced.

DOWN TIME

I sometimes marvel at how little I do
And at how it is necessary for me to do very little.
I could put a flame under myself, perhaps a flicker.
But I have this fire in me to do nothing. And it is important
That a certain amount of time should be reserved
For doing nothing. Both before, during and after
Doing something. And I could be incinerated
By a flicker.

ROOM WITH A VOID

I am not capable, this afternoon, of doing
Anything. It is too hot, and the world -
And all its wives and knives
And children - seems farther away
Than usual. And my own closed quarters
Are closing in on me more oppressively
Than is conducive to the discharging of anything,
Least of all this dimly-perceived notion of duty.

XXXIV

I only take consolation
In other people's failure
In order to feel less lonely.
It is not that I am afraid
Of success. What scares me most
Is the work itself, the required effort:
Of what it will take out of me
And what it will leave me with.

A WEDNESDAY IN AUGUST

I ask little enough of myself,
And I cannot even accomplish that much.
I would rather sit here, obsessively undriven,
Doing as close to nothing as is humanly possible.
Entertaining, occasionally, a pang of grief
Or grievance. Fixing on a stray regret or a memory
Drifting like dust in sunlight, or
A shadow falling over a shadow.

INCANTATION

If I lie on my back I am usually secure
In taking only a short nap, but if I turn
Over, it is all over, and wanton languor insures
The afternoon's demise. Until I find myself blearily reciting
The same exhausted litany of vain exhortations and admonitions
That were recited this time yesterday and will be repeated
This time tomorrow. A matter of clearing the air,
That I might move on and continue to repeat myself.

XXXVII

There have been times, even in my time,
When I have found myself engaged by some
Thing. The end, then, was in sight before
I had even begun. An end that was not
Worked towards. Lazier displeasures
Held more allure, and if anything was achieved,
It was only the very least required to provide
An uneasy satisfaction. Usually, not even that.

THE LAZY STRUGGLE

When I find myself more conscious than I care to be,
My body, unable to bear the strain
Of so much unnaturally imposed sleep,
Begins to rebel against my mind, which, beyond self-reproach
In shabby gluttonous ease, clings to its resting place.
Eventually, corporeal volition asserts itself and I am caught
Unawares, guilt-ridden, groggy and restless,
Left standing on my feet, seeking a different escape.

AN EXPLANATION

I never say that I am working,
Only that I am trying to work.
When, in fact, I am not even trying
To try. I am just sitting here:
Stalling, simmering, sinking.
Getting up every once in a while
To look out of the window
Or to lie down.

TIME MOVES, BUT NOT I

I am no stranger to waste, to bouts of tranquilizing
Self-abuse: drifting off with wilting rod in flowering fist,
Thoughts sliding like water across a pane of glass
And over the edge
Of the sofa and elsewhere. And tension detours
To parts unknown, on days that pass unknown;
Held together by dust,
By boredom and all its blossom.

ELSEWHERE

I may bask in the radiance
Of impending toil. But at the usual place
Of evasion and repetition, when faced
With the possibility of actually executing
My task, I would rather take a nap.
To be within reach of one's goal at last,
Only to turn one's back on it,
Surely there must be some merit in this.

I'M NOT TIRED

It is merely that sitting down to discharge
My duty fills me with queasiness, drains me
Of my will. The act of tying my shoe laces
Overwhelms me. I have to contemplate the veins in my hand for a while.
I have to walk across the room and look out of the window at the empty street,
The empty sunlight. And I have to eat a biscuit and lie down on the sofa,
Where fear and indolence curdle in stagnant repose,
And make myself unknown.

XLIII

I have toyed with some beginnings
But they led nowhere.
My destiny lies in the margins.
If there, if anywhere.
Or beyond them, in that other sphere.
My reputation recedes me,
And an intricately layered indolence
Is my only legacy.

A TIME OF RECKONING

Three o'clock in the afternoon is a difficult time.
My head, were it not supported in my hands,
Would have fallen across the table some time ago.
I could still approach my task. Many hours
Have been squandered in preparation for it.
But it feels natural, somehow right, to drift
In this overfamiliar state, half-asleep with possibilities.
This, after all, is what I do.

LONG STRETCH WITHOUT

Tidal waves of resignation lap up against my chin.
A bead of water strains from a rusty faucet.
Occasional glimpses of clarity and sudden bursts of
Perfervid atrabiliousness punctuate the languid pace of
A routine that chiefly exists in order to deaden the potentially
Disquieting awareness that precisely nothing is being
Achieved. And the afternoon, like so many before,
Trickles away into something spurned, forgotten and unforgiven.

XLVI

Sometimes I wonder why I bother,
And sometimes I wonder why
I don't bother. And I often lament
The fact that nothing I do ever sees
The light of day. Not that I ever do
Anything. But it would be nice
If this absence were not
To pass unnoticed.

ODE TO INVENTED MELANCHOLY

Daunted by the energy that might be unleashed
Were I to concentrate on the supposed task:
Of what it might subtract, exact and adulterate; and of
The gagging staleness that could issue forth, if finally
Penetrated, from something so long suppressed.
Succumbing instead to these afternoons of claustrophobic
Wandering and restless prostration. Committed, only
To non- commitment. Driven, only to distraction.

VIEW FROM A HILL

I am not yet quite over it.
I am lying down on top of it.
Surveying behind me a wasteland
Of dried-up promise.
While the lights below twinkle
With dull mocking uncertainty.
There isn't much left to look forward to,
And the looking forward of the past has been belied.

LYING ON MY SIDE

A trickle of saliva bedews the pillow
Beneath my head. I murmur to myself
In vain: Get up, be a man. Courage,
At the end, will be unavoidable.
Why not have it now?
Forgetting the question, I turn over.
It is four o'clock in the afternoon.
It might as well be four o'clock in the morning.

WATCHING, LISTENING, WAITING

Putting in the time:
Watching: the trembling curtains.
Listening: to the constant hum of indecision.
Waiting: to languish without remorse or hope
Of false dawn; to be able to do nothing
And call it nothing. To sink:
Where I have never sunk before.
To fade, only to be found again.

SEEPAGE

I wish I could be satisfied
Doing nothing, but I can't.
Hence this struggling
Against good fortune
In shallow water.
Adrift, whether still or moving
Nowhere slowly.
As lazy as I am restless.

BORN WINNER, SELF-MADE LOSER

There was a time when I thought
I might have done something by now.
But that was long ago, and over the intervening
Decades I have shifted from prodigy to late-bloomer
To non-bloomer. I have passed my peak without having peaked
Or even begun the ascent, and unless there is something inherently
Salutary to the energy I expend in frustrating myself, then
My sacrifices have all been in vain.

A LONG HARD LAZY APPRENTICESHIP

You would think by now that people would know better
Than to ask me what I have been doing with my time.
And you would think by now that I would have come up
With an answer that would silence them. But I still stumble,
Crumble and quail when faced with this thankless enquiry.
I suppose I could tell them the truth: that after all the brooding,
Abstraction and evasion, there just isn't much time left
To do the work, or to tell the truth.

CHAIR, SOFA AND BED

Between these three points of love
And sloth (Mostly the latter),
I flounder. Resting, without laurels,
Restlessly. Pausing between pauses
To inventory this harvest of regret;
To consider, from every angle of unease,
This permanent rut... to forever name remainless,
Staring at a curtain.

IMPROVIDENCE

The other lives I might have led
All now might as well be
Dead. Survived by no one.
Barren, without issue of any sort:
This withered bud, failed
In art and love. With no time left
To change my course. But time enough
For infinite remorse.

LIFELONG LEAN PERIOD

I have been awake since the dawn of noon,
And I have nothing to show for the time that
Was mine. To begin with I never began.
I sat down at the table with vaguely creditable intentions
But they were soon replaced by mere struggle
To remain awake, and with all the energy I could muster
I relocated to the sofa, where, several drowsified hours later,
I begin to chastise myself again.

DUST FALLS REGARDLESS

I once took solace in comparing myself to other
Malingerers. Until it became clear that my lack
Of progress eclipsed even the most laggardly
Among them, and that there remained no sign,
At this precarious hour, of the most rudimentary
Beginning. At which point it also became clear
That I cannot compare myself to anyone
Who has done anything.

THAT TIME OF DAY

A destructive overawareness of time
Knives through the hot empty spaces
Of an afternoon. A sense of urgency vaporizing
Into torpor. Even the traffic sounds tired.
Do something, I tell myself.
What? The same thing I've been doing
Every day for years on end
With varying degrees of failure.

INURED TO OTIOSITY

I am told, often enough, that it is not too late
To do something with my life.
But, unfortunately, the fact that I am not dead yet
Fails to inspire much hope or motivation
For a productive future. And on the evidence of my past
It is clear that there will be no belated burst of activity.
I have been talking about last hurrahs for a long time,
Without any sign of an initial hurrah.

LX

I am a great believer in half measures
Or no measures at all. And I am a great champion
Of dishonest suffering, false modesty and vain inhibitions.
When the problem, painful to admit, is pure
Laziness: punishing myself for doing nothing
By doing nothing. I am often informed that I have nobody
To blame but myself - as if any comfort might be derived
From this cruelly stated fact.

LXI

In darkness slowly awakening
To what I have not always known:
That it is too late in the day or the lifetime
To change course or return, with
Any stainless sense of purpose, to the dream.
The notion that I might ever accomplish anything
Remains confined to dusty imagination
And when I close my eyes, it is still too bright.

THE WORLD IS MY WIDOW

It was an afterthought that brought me here
Towards the end of another idle afternoon
That spits me out spent. I made it
As far as the sofa - anchorage of undertow
And arid equivocation. - Awaking from a dream
Into another dream; glimpsing the passing notion
That being awake, too, might have its pleasures, its rewards.
And relatively alert again, I reanesthetize myself.

ACCOMPLISHMENT

It would be a relief if I could resign myself
To unproductivity and simply exist
Unburdened by this tiresome need to produce
That has been the cause of so much unpleasantness.
It's not as if I do anything with my time
And as for most of the people who do accomplish
Anything: One rather wishes they hadn't bothered either.
Accomplishment, I suspect, is overrated.

CREATION

I have been sitting here,
Gritting my teeth in the hot light of day,
For what seems a long time
But probably isn't.
I cannot do what I want to do
And I cannot do anything else.
A lamentable waste, but the absence of this
Emptiness would create an immense yawning void in my life.

DAYS

Mornings are spent preparing for activity.
Nights are spent recovering from inactivity.
Why torment myself over succumbing
To an inertia so inevitable that I could set my clock
By the onslaught of it? Why not just accept it?
To do otherwise is only an exercise
In frustration: a phrase that could easily apply
To my entire life.

A PRELUDE OF SORTS

For years I have tarried, secure
In the notion that all this luxuriating
In vicarious decay served some sort of purpose. Until
It became apparent that this extended arid preamble
Had turned terminal, squashing any prospect
Of fecundity. Fading without ever having flourished;
A dream unwinding, grinding
To a standstill.

ANOTHER DAY

Take some initiative,
Do something with your life:
I get up from the sofa,
Walk across to the table
And write these words
Down on a scrap of paper.
Then I return to the sofa
And fall asleep.

HOW LITTLE, HOW FAR

I have never done less:
I keep saying this
And yet I keep outdoing myself.
One would assume
That one would have to do something
To get from morning to night.
But I have proven that this
Is not necessarily the case.

CRABWISE

The day stretches out before me,
Rich in infinite possibility,
Collapses on itself, rolls over,
And flattens into immobility.
One day these days will all be over.
What am I going to do
Between now and then?
I haven't decided yet.

NO GREAT DISTANCE

This is the season you looked ahead to, the later days,
By which time, you imagined, some measure
Of satisfaction might have been attained.
And this is how far you have come.
You assumed, incorrectly,
That you would eventually get around to doing something
With your life, that there would be some reward for all this.
For what? For all this frustration.

LIVING PROOF

There are those who excuse all the wasted days
And nights and years (that were not theirs) by claiming
That if one were meant to have been doing something
During that time, then one would have done it.
They are reluctant, for some reason, to acknowledge
That there is such a thing as 'a waste of time':
A phrase so ubiquitous in my life
That it has become meaningless.

WASTED MORNING

I woke up this afternoon
And sneered at the clock,
At this invention that will dictate
The all too predictable frustrations
Of the day. I remained where I was,
Stifling any potentially misleading
Signs of vitality, deadening myself
Before I even got out of bed.

THE LIFE OF THE MIND

Here I must remain, lost
In a closed world of disorder, studying
And smothering the frantic underpinnings
Of my lassitude. Pausing, now and then,
To take stock of my lack of activity,
My varying states of immobility.
Considering giving up.
Then giving up.

CONSTANCY

Out of this boredom nothing can emerge,
For all has merged into it. All hope and sensation
Accedes to its creation. Perfectionism itself
Becomes an excuse to do nothing... and solitude
Is just another form of laziness: the freedom to drift
Unchecked and unencumbered, when you can't drift
Anymore, and when you have forgotten
How to do anything but drift.

MISEMPLOYMENT

I have already put in more than my share
Of time that adds up to nothing:
One afternoon after another passing
In a hypnagogic blur, struggling
To find it's just not there. Trapped
In a refuge of bypassed intentions.
Yet from this tedium
I would not welcome interruption.

LEADEN AFTERNOON

On the threshold of execution:
An urgent need degenerates into a chimera,
A hideous abstraction, an impossibility
Within my grasp. I consider it for a moment:
There is nothing in the air.
I let it grow heavier and drag me down.
Because if I remain here I will have to do something,
And that might not be possible.

LXXVII

Always the thought of time running out:
Always more time. It passes quickly
Due to lack of change or care. Always there,
As if it had never been. There is never as much
As there was: to evade, absorb,
Accumulate and rue the loss of;
To ponder how it moves
And will one day move without me.

FIVE O'CLOCK

My workday is drawing to a close.
It lasted twenty minutes. But it is already clear
That I am not going to do anything further
On this particular day. I could push myself,
I suppose, if I felt capable of pushing myself.
But I don't feel capable of it. And if I did,
I probably wouldn't push myself. I would probably
Do something less rewarding.

FEAR OF KNOWN THINGS

For a long time I have succeeded
In avoiding reality.
It has remained on the rim
Of my existence, slowly spinning, kept
At a respectful distance;
Accepted, feared but never faced,
Supplanted by a jangled state
Of grace.

LXXX

I like to complain.
It creates the illusion
That I'm doing something.
But I can't complain,
Therefore I have nothing
To say. And nothing seems worth saying.
Yet I sit here trying to pretend
Otherwise... or otherwise.

FROM PILLAR TO PILLOW

Every day is a journey
From hidden hope to resignation;
From honorable intention
To blurred self-flagellation.
But there comes a point
When it is easier to do one's work
Than agonize about not doing it.
I haven't reached that point yet.

SELF DISCOVERY

It is shocking to discover
Exactly how little I do.
But perhaps these marathon
Bouts of leisurely frustration
And nervous wriggling distraction
Should be viewed as a sacrifice
Or an investment that must be made in order
That the slightest profit might be yielded.

YELLOW AFTERNOON OF THE SOUL

I am reliant upon spurts
That soon sputter out. The slightest diligence
Unleashes a heightened awareness
Of my own existence... my own innocence... this precious life...
I want to stop; it has to simmer down
To a manageable boredom. And with this desire for composure,
Fear of death and torpor merge in an unlikely union
That bears no fruit.

REMAINS

I lie awake on grainy mornings,
Gently killing the hours
Of causeless hope, dozing
Without reason and numbing myself
To the numbness of what will be left
Of this new day, by the time I finally rise
And the crooked struggle begins
To remain awake.

LXXXV

There are no levees capable
Of withstanding the torrents of distraction
That surge through my mind. Tender
Resentments, useless trivia and tired lusts
Are carried along like debris on a swollen river,
From which, very occasionally, a lucid thought
Emerges, only to be sucked back down
Into the sewage of pettiness and vanity.

FROM CONDUIT TO CIPHER

For too long a conduit I have been,
Receptive only to the works of others.
In this way, in a way, I have kept myself
Going; and were it not for the pleasure
And enrichment I receive at this font,
I might long ago have given up.
Then again, I might have
Achieved something myself.

AT A LOSS

I cannot proceed naturally. On the verge
Of the verge of application, I become too conscious
Of finally vaguely making progress to make any further
Progress. The awareness that I could be doing more
Prevents me from doing anything at all. I am unwilling
To lose myself, to face that which is already lost or that
Which remains to be lost, and I confront once more
The only thing I am capable of creating: a blockage.

THE WAGES OF SLOTH

That which I should have got out of my system years ago
Is still in my so-called system, only buried deeper than ever.
And the strength, ability and desire to unearth it
Have all dwindled. The years have all passed by,
The years that could have been spent wisely.
And how were they tortured into submission,
What happened? What markers can be used
To navigate my way back through such a vacuum?

BENEATH MYSELF

Anything that requires perseverence
Has a wilting effect upon me.
When opportunity calls,
Apathy is the natural response.
I cannot even call myself a failure.
I have never tried hard enough
At anything
To earn even that accolade.

MY BRILLIANT NON-CAREER

I often tell myself that I could have done anything
I applied myself to. When, out of all the things I could have
Applied myself to, I applied myself to doing nothing.
And found that I couldn't even do that.
The notion that I should have been doing something
Kept getting in the way.
And now, of course, it is too late
To do anything: It has always been too late.

ANOTHER DAZE, ANOTHER DOLOR

I am not going to get anything done today.
It is a fact, impure and deniable,
Written in shadow, but more definite
Than anything else in my life. It is as if I were restrained
By some unseen force. For there must be other forces
At work. I cannot accept sole responsibility
For such pain-killing impotence. I cannot believe myself
Capable of something so conclusive.

XCII

I can't settle anywhere, on anything.
Yet I remain here,
As if I will always be here, getting nowhere,
Waning prosaically, stretching myself
Towards a dead-end:
Carrying on as if I'm going to live forever,
As if inactivity itself were an activity: a denial
Of mortality.

XCIII

My days are short
And strenuously idle;
A tapestry of vagueness
Spread thin and frayed
With agitation. While the carpet
Far below resembles a desert landscape:
Tumbleweeds of hair, and dust
That falls like rain.

LIFE WITHOUT WORK

To do nothing
In this day and age,
When so much pointless work
Is being produced,
Could almost be considered an achievement.
It all compares most unfavorably
With my own imaginary
Body of work.

ROMANCE WITH FAILURE

I have wandered in the darkness, within and without,
But I can't bring myself to walk in the light
That one hears so much about.
Somehow it just wouldn't seem right
To stray from the romance with failure
I have long held dear: an affair
that should have ended many years ago.
But a futile fidelity still holds me there.

ESTIVATION

Throughout the summer
There haven't been many breezes
In the exterior world. Day after day,
Just folding over. My mind not moving.
Bowed down and undetermined,
Picking at scabs of time. Given the choice
Between stark panic and dull suspense,
I have taken the latter.

LOOK BACK IN LANGUOR

It is strange to consider
That I once actually had a future.
And It is becoming difficult to look back
With any pleasure upon my past. A lostness
Washes through me, freighted with bitter nostalgia.
I am reminded of a time of hope that never materialized.
And I find that the past itself has become tainted
By the future.

XCVIII

What became of the last half hour?
It was obliterated by lamentation.
It was consumed by thoughts
Of what should have been,
And what shouldn't have been,
And what wasn't. And what
Became of the last quarter of a century?
Much the same.

OVERUNDEREXTENSION

I have nothing to say,
And I don't know why
I feel obliged to say anything at all.
Yet I sit here straining
In a void, if that: a bloodless and farcical straining.
While deluding myself that there is anything within
That bears bringing to the light of day,
Or that could bear that light.

WORK ETHIC

I cannot break through the barriers
Of self-consciousness and sleepiness
Induced by too much sleep. But I insist
Upon remaining here for another hour,
Even if nothing comes of it: a slackening
Sentence of sorts - toiling not but still
Spinning. My capacity for boredom
Disturbs me, as does my ability to endure it.

CI

I am trying to improve my attitude.
But my attitude keeps deteriorating.
I am afraid of getting lost
In anything positive, for that would require
An altogether alien kind of energy,
Of which I am wary:
For it might furnish urgent proof
Of life, of death, of feeling.

CITADEL

Am I empty at the core or just around the edges?
Are there riches therein? I wouldn't know.
I'm weighed down in a warm white glow,
Crushing the stark yellow dullness of the day
Into dust, statically and statelessly drifting
Throughout this haze of rust. Riding the waves
Of lostness across the landscape of a desk,
Into the bulwark of a threadbare curtain.

RECOGNIZABLE REALITY

It is mildly unsettling to discover
That I am not observing my life,
I am actually living it: in denial, as best I can.
I don't want to know how I'm doing.
Perhaps I would be better off facing reality.
But it's been a long time and I might not recognize it.
Perhaps this is reality. It might as well be.
Why not?

CIV

Faced with beauty, I see only fate
Falling into place:
The tenderness of waste
And the infinite loss that I embraced.
Who will know these things?
The spheres immersed in, the deep inner richness
Of my existence, the rest, unrest,
The restlessness... and all the rest.

CV

I tried, to no avail, to rot.
I really gave it my best shot.
But vitality kept getting in the way, appearing
Unexpectedly, when I was most hopeful
Of abandoning hope.
But still I refuse to give up
On giving up. I remain optimistic
That I still have it in me.

CVI

Contact with anybody
Who has produced work of quality
Fills me with an air of thwarted yearning empathy,
An implausible sense of fraternity,
A melancholy sting. Regret and resentment
Gnawing at me, eating me alive.
This is what you reap
When you haven't sown anything.

CVII

With my love
In my cold, old, dry hands,
I privatize my urges; launching myself
Into blank interiority, falling into shapelessness;
All the remaining energy leaves my body.
It is strenuous, abrasive and draining work.
And it is beginning to feel absurd in a way that it never did before.
Perhaps even this uninspired pleasure will be denied me as I grow old.

AGITATION PEAK, INERTIA VALLEY

The leaves tremble against the window.
I envy and resent them.
But perhaps they too are silently agitated.
It's hard to tell: I don't move much either. I dwell
In distraction, sidetracked by one thing after another:
By nothing. Anywhere, it seems, would be fresher
Than here. But I could infect anywhere
With my own staleness.

SOMETHING

I have spent my entire life
Preparing to do something
That I am never going to do.
I thought that accumulating
All this learning and experience
Would result in something: a body of work…
Or a body. While neglecting to take into account
That I might actually have to do something to achieve that end.

CX

I find it hard to live
In the moment:
For the moment, for the moment,
Is lost on me. Pleasurable sensation
Serves only as fuel for future consolation.
I don't care about experience any more:
I don't need any more experience,
And I don't need any more memories either.

CXI

I have erected a barrier between myself and reality,
Behind which unclaimed moments
Leave a vacuum of harried boredom.
I have a dim memory
Of having once flickered more forcefully.
But it's hard to tell when one is losing it:
When there's nothing left to measure it against.
It's gone.

CXII

Is there any point in sitting here at all:
Courting luck without design; stretching out
A dry spell; groggily awaiting the occasional spark;
Comforting myself in the knowledge
Of what I imagine I'm capable of,
While watching my capabilities slipping by;
Satisfying myself that I can't sink any lower.
Then, sinking lower.

CXIII

There's no point forcing it.
I've been forcing it for long enough:
Going through the motions, motionlessly,
Directionlessly, pleasurelessly. Attempting
Is no longer tempting. Other than to furnish myself
With further proof of incapacity, there doesn't seem
To be much point in trying anymore. Maybe I can give up after all.
I should never have underestimated my ability in that area.

THE MEASURE OF A MAN

A long time ago I made a decision
To become a failure. It wasn't
As easy as I thought: browsing through life
From one distraction to the next, while waiting
For the last lost moment to become unseizable.
As if there were some fundamental honesty
To not striving: There wasn't.
I suspected it all along.

CONATION

I refuse to give up
For at least another half hour.
And if, by then, I still haven't
Produced anything, will this time
Still count? And what will it count as?
Can exertion that produces nothing
Be rewarded, or even recognized?
Can it even be counted as exertion?

PATRONAGE OF NEGATION

I am constantly confronted by other people's works
That I could have created myself.
And I am constantly disappointed by them.
Sadly, I have to recognize them
For what they are: inferior versions
Of what I could have done
If I'd been insecure enough in my abilities
To do anything.

CXVII

Now that it has arrived, this long craved moment
Of supposedly functioning, I find that I cannot do
Anything with it. For in addition to the numerous days
That I take full responsibility for the forfeiture of,
There are other days simply unsuited for endeavor,
Days when certain atmospheric conditions prevail:
A climate of hopelessness, against which it is useless to struggle,
And equally useless to surrender to.

CXVIII

I feel as if I don't have time
To do anything. So I do nothing
Other than remind myself
Of what I should be doing,
And admonish myself for not doing it.
I tell myself to be patient.
But I don't have time for patience anymore.
I don't have time for time.

DONE

Now I understand how things are done.
How I didn't do things,
How I never will.
What's undone is done
And what's done is undone.
Can one remain promising for as long
As one's promise remains unfulfilled?
Can one be posthumously promising?

CXX

Time spent alone, to others unknown:
Black and white afternoons,
Sallow evenings and discolored nights
Spent grasping for distraction;
Glancing at moments
That could have been savored -
That will disappear, unaccounted for, forgotten,
Along with everything else, even by myself.

CXXI

They pain me, such days as these,
When, gripped by the murkiness
Of a certain deadly coziness, relishing
The state of semi-consciousness at the darkening
Of another tedious shift of exhausting agitation,
It occurs to me, once again, that over the course of this day
I have made no contribution to anybody else's life.
I haven't even made a contribution to my own life.

TO POSTERITY

My most profound observations
Have gone unrecorded. They were too subtle
And I was too lazy to pin them down.
I was always sluggishly scrambling
On to the next thing that would remain undone
Or underdone. It was, of course, within my power
To formulate them, despite the fact
That no evidence of them exists.

FORCED INTO OPTIMISM

I have finally reached the stage
Where optimism, glimpsed from afar,
Seems viable - even, sadly, imperative.
A disturbing prospect: that desperate
Optimism, derided as the fuel
For other people's lives.
I only hope that I won't be carried along by it
Into anything resembling permanence.

CXXIV

It was not meant for me to fail.
It doesn't feel right. But it is
What I have chosen to undo
With my life, what I have unmade
Of myself. It is disturbing that I am prepared
To settle for so little: only promise. But perhaps
There never really was a time of promise.
I've always felt past my prime.

STEPPING OUT

Another day lies squandered behind me.
The effluvia of recent useless vacillation
Pollutes my abode and suffocates my higher faculties.
I seek relief from the nausea of my own society
In the outside world.
To reward myself with distraction:
Not for work well done, or done at all
But as relief from tormenting myself over not doing the work.

CXXVI

How good it feels
At the end of such a long stale day
Of sedentary agitation; a relief
From the restraints of restlessness:
To walk forth in relatively fresh air and recognize anew
That the concept that everything is possible
Can be grasped
Theoretically.

ADDENDA

When one prioritizes doing nothing
one's time becomes very precious.

You reap what you sow
and so on.

Annoyed by the sun,
I sought refuge in a moist pillow.

For optimism I lack the vigor.

a plane groans across the sky
and the traffic's diminishing roar
collapses into silence
on this barren shore,
These shallows where I have chosen to founder,

Precision-timed work avoidance
is what constitutes the rigid order of my days,

Preparing new ways to enliven dead rituals
and discounting them
Sucked down into the swelter

These long afternoons that enter my life without morning.

While drying up.

It is hard to give up
giving up. It is hard to give.

Rise and chastise.

Many unrealized revelations, many unacted upon breakthroughs later.

I have nothing to show for my dissatisfaction.

living in the present, negligibly;
regretting the past, sweepingly;
and speculating upon the future,
incredulously.

Somebody else's passing stupor is my fixed reality.

A sun behind the clouds, a circle of light quivering upon the floor.

With so much unfinished, so much unbegun.

I'm not in the mood
for anything.

I have sacrificed everything for the work.
But I haven't done the work.

Devoted to obscurity.

To live, between periods of unconsciousness, with dead time.

In a continual stricken hurry to do nothing.

A hard day's shirk, eking out a loafing.

The rigid order of my days resulting in nothing like discipline.

A license to kill time.

This time-consuming desire to do nothing.

A few moments of genuine concentration are more than I can stand. before everything must become fuzzy again.

All I already haven't done.

The day, without starting, has drawn to a close.

I crave stillness and symmetry;
I crave a soothing emptiness
and mistake it for clarity.

It is just a matter of putting in the time.
But what if I put nothing into the time?

I require Something definite
to vacillate about.

Time that will never be attested to, hours that came to naught.

I am too content
to drift uncomfortably,
desultorily, on waves
of bleariness... nowhere
in particular, out of fidelity
to nothing in particular.

What would happen if I made an honest effort? Probably nothing.

Everything has to proceed at a certain pacelessness.
Otherwise I don't trust it.

I don't work well under pressure... or without pressure.

Inactivity breeds impure thoughts.

I cannot function during the afternoon.
Nor do I flourish at any other time.

Six months to me are as six days to somebody more active...
to somebody that does almost anything.

To struggle without doing anything.

The silence in my ears is getting louder.
Perhaps it signals the approach of death.

I haven't officially given up yet

This precious paralysis.

To seek distraction is to do something.

Hope seems hollow and Sleep without reason.

the furniture is still flickering

Ah, to be old and unsuccessful.

To meet reality halfway... or not at all... or not at all.

I have issues with the arrangement of time.

immovably restless,
clinging to the vagueness,
a clammy glutinous vagueness

I merely rebel against the expenditure of energy, the effort involved.

But conscious... and that in itself signifies
Some vague victory.

A vow of indolence.

luxuriating in ambiguities,
soon it will be too late for such concerns

So long have I been sitting here and so little have I done.

It is not coming easily. I cannot allow it
to come easily. I cannot allow it to come at all.

Nothing will ever attest to this time.

Hive of inactivity.

the pointless battles fought,
imaginary breakthroughs that came to naught.

Failure goes to my head.

Aftershocks, napping troughs.

I don't like to work hard, even at what I enjoy doing.

I was waiting for the right moment. I realize now that it is unlikely to ever come.

The sun is murder.

Wouldn't mind the slowness if it meant eventually getting somewhere.

Destiny unarrowed.

Just lying there.

Struggling to stop struggling.

So much time stretching towards a dead-end.

Indecision upon indecision.

Unnatural rest.

captivity

I just got up
and now I'm going
to lie down somewhere else.

Sapped signs of life.

To live in constant eclipse.

With so much unfinished, so much unbegun.

Moving things around on a table,
Staring at my hand.

Dedicated to Forfeiture of Accomplishment.

As I have been saying for a long time, there is still time.

Shirk ethic.

I'm stuck here at this table
and

Panic sets in, but apathy wins the day.

I'm twice the failure you'll ever be.

Struggling with the temptation
to give up struggling.

Determined
to give up.

I suppose I'd rather be consumed
with regret.

as if enduring massive inconsequential frustration
were an acceptable substitute for the satisfaction
of actual work.

Impenetrable blur.

I don't have it in me.

Brief bursts - not even bursts -
Of activity - not even activity.

Many unacted upon breakthroughs, many unrealized
revelations later.

Tis' wealth enough for one day.

Just sitting there.

A guttered candle... specks floating in the air.

of my flow... my stasis

John Tottenham was born.....

He is not available.

Made in the USA
Lexington, KY
03 December 2013